Documents for Democracy

Building America and Literacy Skills Through Primary Sources

Volume 1: 17th and 18th Centuries

**Prepared by
Veronica Burchard
Illustrations by Courtney Burrough**

Dedicated to my loving husband,
Kyle Burchard,
as well as my mentor and friend,
Claire McCaffery Griffin

Edited by Matthew F. Galella
Design and typography by Graham Communications

ISBN-13: 978-0-9817616-9-5

Printed in the United States of America
December 2009

Visit **www.aihe-bookstore.com**

Table of Contents

John Winthrop's

City Upon A Hill

You may wish to emphasize to students that although the *City Upon a Hill* sermon is religious in nature, you will not be presenting it as truth. Rather, you will be reading it as a way of understanding this period in history.

Lines leading up to the passage where this abridged document begins:

We are entered into covenant with Him. … We have hereupon besought Him of favor and blessing … but if we shall neglect the observation of these articles which are the ends we have propounded, and, dissembling with our God, shall fall to embrace this present world and prosecute our carnal intentions, seeking great things for ourselves and our posterity, the Lord will surely break out in wrath against us, and be revenged of such a people, and make us know the price of the breach of such a covenant.

Notes: _____

_____

_____

_____

_____

_____

_____

_____

_____

_____

_____

_____

_____

_____

Introduction

Almost 400 years ago, a group of people called the Puritans lived in England. The Puritans wanted to live by their own religious beliefs. They decided to leave England and settle across the Atlantic Ocean in the New World. Their settlement would be called the Massachusetts Bay Colony.

John Winthrop

John Winthrop was elected governor of the Massachusetts Bay Colony. As the Puritans got ready to cross the Atlantic in 1630, Winthrop wanted to encourage them. He explained their duty to obey God, and that as long as they did, God would bless them. This agreement was called a covenant. Winthrop also told the Puritans that their new colony would be an example for all the world to see. If they succeeded, the whole world would admire them. If they failed, the whole world would see that, too.

Although Winthrop was speaking to the Puritans of his time, his words about America serving as an example to the world have lived on. Many believe the United States continues to be an example of hope and justice for the whole world.

What Is a Primary Source?

A primary source is a piece of history. It is a document from a time period, like a diary, a speech, a newspaper article, or a photograph. In this chapter, you will study the sermon **City Upon a Hill** as a primary source from 1630, as a way to learn about that time period of American history. This document is religious in nature. You will read it because understanding the religious beliefs of the time is important to learning about this period in history.

_____

_____

_____

_____

Activating Prior Knowledge:
Questions for Pre-Reading Discussion

1. What do you know about the groups of people who left England for the New World in the 1600s?

2. Have you ever heard of the Puritans? What do you know about them?

3. Have you ever been unhappy in a place or situation — so unhappy that you wanted to leave?

4. The Puritans wanted to be role models for others. Have you ever been a role model? How would you describe that experience?

Vocabulary and Context Questions

Complete this page as you read. Using context clues and/or a dictionary, define each word:

Vocabulary

Avoid:	*stay away from*
Posterity:	*our children, and our children's children*
Humbly:	*respectfully, not proudly*
Entertain:	*treat each other*
Meekness:	*submissiveness, with no resistance*
Liberality:	*generosity*
Unity:	*oneness*
Consider:	*take into account*
Withdraw:	*take away*
Perish:	*die*
Whither:	*whether or not*
Cleaving:	*remaining firmly and loyally*

Context Questions

1. Who gave this speech? *John Winthrop, the governor-elect of the Massachusetts Bay Colony*

2. What was his purpose? *To emphasize the colonists' special covenant with God; to remind them that if they were faithful and obedient to God, God would bless them, and by contrast God would withdraw help if they were disobedient*

3. Who was listening to him (or whom did he want to hear it)? *The Puritan Massachusetts Bay colonists. Some students might say he hoped that officials of the Church of England would hear about it too, as the Puritans wished to reform the Church of England.*

4. When did he give this speech? *1630*

Supplementary Information

- The Puritans could no longer tolerate the practices of the Church of England. John Winthrop wrote about their decision to establish a colony in the New World: "the Church [of England] hath no place left to fly into but the wilderness" (*Reasons for the Plantation in New England*, ca 1628).

- Winthrop says the reason for the voyage to America is "to seek out a place of cohabitation and consortship under a due form of government both civil and ecclesiastical." Church and state, to use modern terms, would not be separate.

- Unlike the Pilgrims who settled Plymouth Colony in 1620, the Puritans remained nominally a part of the Church of England, and hoped to reform it from within.

- The Winthrop fleet was made up of 11 ships with about 700 passengers.

- It was long thought that John Winthrop gave this sermon aboard the *Arbella*, though many historians now believe it was delivered in England before leaving for the New World.

- Winthrop's *City Upon a Hill* sermon is also known by its full title *A Model of Christian Charity*.

Comprehension and Discussion Questions

- What does Winthrop mean by "shipwreck"? Is he talking about their boat actually sinking? *No, he is speaking metaphorically: the "shipwreck" refers to the disaster that would result if the Puritans did not follow their*

The only way to avoid this shipwreck and to provide for our posterity is to do justly, to love mercy, to walk humbly with our God.

God's word.

- What three things does Winthrop tell the settlers they must do? "*... do justly, love mercy, and walk humbly with their God.*"

Notes: _____

_____

_____

We must be knit together in this work as one man, we must entertain each other in brotherly affection.

Supplementary Information

- Puritans believed that all members of a Christian community were part of a body. Different parts had different purposes, but no part was more vital than any other. Differences among people were natural and ordained by their God: "The condition of mankind, as in all times some must be rich, some poor, some high and eminent in power and dignity; others mean and in submission." These differences gave people the chance to act charitably and lovingly, in ways that

glorified their God.

Comprehension and Discussion Questions

- How does Winthrop say the colonists should treat each other? *With "brotherly affection," in other words with kindness and courtesy, and genuine love.*

- Why does Winthrop say the colonists should "knit together" as one person? *They should be united or bonded together.*

- Can you think of examples of this idea in your life? *Students may suggest marriage (their parents are a unit); brothers, sisters and parents and extended family members making up one family; bonds of friendship that are defined by unity and loyalty: "All for one and one for all."*

Notes: _____

_____

_____

_____

_____

_____

_____

_____

_____

_____

_____

_____

_____

_____

_____

Supplementary Information

- The emphasis on "together" demonstrates how Puritans saw their destinies as intertwined. As their God's favored people, Puritans were chosen for salvation. Their experiences on Earth were one as well. They thought good works, while not necessary for salvation, would help them avoid plagues, natural disasters, and other earthly forms of their God's wrath.

- In another passage of *A Model of Christian Charity*, Winthrop expanded on the idea of suffering together: "If one member suffers, all suffer with it, if one be in honor, all rejoice with it."

Comprehension and Discussion Questions

- What values does Winthrop encourage in this part of his sermon? *Meekness, gentleness, patience, liberality, and unity (being and doing "together.").*

- Do you ever share happiness or sadness with others? How does that change the experience of those feelings? *Answers will vary. Students may say that sharing happiness with others makes them feel happier, while sharing sadness can make people feel not as sad anymore.*

- Why do you think Winthrop thought the colonists should share all these things? *Because it will strengthen their bonds of community, and help them keep their covenant with God. Just as their experiences on Earth were tied together, so was their standing in God's eyes.*

Together in all meekness, gentleness, patience and liberality, we must delight in each other, mourn together, labor, and suffer together.

Notes: _____

_____

_____

_____

_____

Always having before our eyes ... our community as members of the same body, so shall we keep the unity of the spirit in the bond of peace, the Lord will command a blessing upon us in all our ways.

elaborates on the idea of the members of the community as part of the same body, knit together by love: "Love is the bond of perfection. First it is a bond or ligament. Secondly, it makes the work perfect. There is no body but consists of parts and that which knits these parts together, gives the body its perfection. It makes each part so contiguous to others as thereby they do mutually participate with each other, both in strength and infirmity, in pleasure and pain."

Comprehension and Discussion Questions

- What three values does Winthrop mention in this part of his sermon? *Community, unity, and peace.*

- How do spirits of community and unity promote peace? *Because they see themselves as part of the same "body," the Puritans know they have a common goal and will work together harmoniously.*

- What does Winthrop tell the colonists that their God will give them? *Blessing.*

Notes: _____

_____

_____

_____

_____

_____

_____

_____

Supplementary Information

- The Puritans believed nations had a covenant with their God. Some communities had broken their covenant with disobedience and sinful behavior, which had caused their God to withdraw His favor. This passage shows Puritans' belief in their own covenant with their God, and Winthrop's hope for its success: "... the Lord will command a blessing upon us ..."

- In another passage of *A Model of Christian Charity*, Winthrop

Supplementary Information

- John Winthrop was paraphrasing from the Bible. In the Sermon on the Mount, Jesus Christ said: *"You are the light of the world. A city set on a mountain cannot be hidden. Nor do they light a lamp and then put it under a bushel basket; it is set on a lampstand, where it gives light to all in the house. Just so, your light must shine before others, that they may see your good deeds and glorify your heavenly Father."*

- Presidents John F. Kennedy and Ronald Reagan quoted this passage of *A Model of Christian Charity*.

Comprehension and Discussion Questions

- John Winthrop says that the "the eyes of all people" will be on the Puritan community. Have you ever been a role model for someone else? *Answers will vary, but students may say they are role models for younger siblings or cousins, for younger schoolmates, for others within civic organizations like Boy Scouts or Girl Scouts, within athletic teams, or within their religious communities.*

- How did that make you feel? *Answers will vary.*

- How do you think the Puritans felt when they heard these words? *They were probably filled with a sense of holy duty, or a special sense of unique responsibility. They might have been frightened, but worked to find courage.*

For we must consider that we shall be as a City Upon a Hill, the eyes of all people are upon us.

Notes: _____

_____

_____

_____

_____

_____

So if we deal falsely with our God in this work we shall cause him to withdraw his present help from us. We shall be made a story through the world.

If our hearts shall turn away, so that we will not obey, we shall surely perish out of the good land whither we pass over this vast sea to possess it.

Supplementary Information

- This passage illustrates what the Puritans believe happens to nations who are not faithful to their God. They believed their God withdraws help and favor from those nations, for all to see. They will fail as a community, and may suffer plagues or other natural disasters.

- In another passage from *City Upon a Hill*, Winthrop says that if the colonists are disobedient, "the Lord will surely break out in wrath against us" and their God will "be revenged."

Comprehension and Discussion Questions

- What does Winthrop say will happen to the colonists if they are not faithful to their God? *Their God will take away the assistance they now have from Him.*

- What does he mean by "we shall be made a story through the world"? *All the world can see the city upon the hill — whether it succeeds or fails.*

- Do your parents or teachers ever "make an example" of someone? What does that mean? *When an authority figure uses the actions of one person to demonstrate to others the consequences (good or bad) of those actions.*

- What is the "vast sea" Winthrop refers to? *The Atlantic Ocean.*

- How would you describe this "covenant" the Puritans believed they had? *They promised to be faithful and obedient, and their God would bless and show favor toward them. If the Puritans held up their "end of the bargain," their community would be a success and would glorify their God. If they were disobedient, however, their God would punish them, and they would die.*

Notes: _____

_____

_____

_____

_____

_____

_____

_____

Supplemental Information

- These are the closing lines of Winthrop's sermon.

- Of the original 700 people in Winthrop's fleet, about 200 died during the first year. About 100 more people returned to England the next spring. But by the end of the 1630s, more than 20,000 Puritans lived in the colony.

- More than 50,000 people came to the New World from England in the Great Migration. (The separatist Pilgrims had established the Plymouth Colony in 1620).

- About 10 years later, in 1641, the colony adopted the Massachusetts Body of Liberties, one of the first two governing documents in the colonies, and a significant precursor to the United States Constitution.

Comprehension and Discussion Questions

- What does Winthrop urge the colonists to do? *To "choose life," or choose to obey their God.*

- What does he mean by "our seed"? *Future generations.*

- Does the sermon end on a discouraging note, or a hopeful one? *Answers will vary.*

Notes: _____

_____

_____

_____

_____

_____

Therefore let us choose life, that we and our seed may live, by obeying His voice and cleaving to Him, for He is our life and our prosperity.

_____

_____

_____

_____

City Upon a Hill

The only way to avoid this shipwreck
and to provide for our posterity is to do justly,
to love mercy, to walk humbly with our God.

We must be knit together in this work as one man,
we must entertain each other in brotherly affection.

Together in all meekness, gentleness, patience and
liberality, we must delight in each other,
mourn together, labor, and suffer together.

Always having before our eyes our community
as members of the same body, so shall we keep the
unity of the spirit in the bond of peace, the Lord
will command a blessing upon us in all our ways.

For we must consider that we shall be as a
City Upon a Hill, the eyes of all people are upon us.

So if we deal falsely with our God in this work we
shall cause him to withdraw his present help from
us. We shall be made a story through the world.
If our hearts shall turn away, so that we will not
obey, we shall surely perish out of the good land
whither we pass over this vast sea to possess it.

Therefore let us choose life, that we and
our seed may live, by obeying His voice
and cleaving to Him, for He is
our life and our prosperity.

Wrap-up Discussion Questions

- How do you think the Puritans felt while they listened to *City Upon a Hill?*

- Which parts of the sermon do you think made them feel hopeful? Which parts might have made them feel scared?

- Why do you think Americans remember this speech 400 years later (and U.S. presidents have quoted it through history)?

- Do you think John Winthrop would make a good teacher, coach, or other leader?

- What qualities seem most important to these early colonists?

- Are these important qualities for Americans to value today? Why or why not?

- The Puritans believed they had a covenant with their God. What other kinds of covenants can you think of — in your family? in sports you play? with friends?

- Do you think America is still a "city upon a hill"? Explain.

American Institute
FOR HISTORY EDUCATION
"Well done is better than well said"

© 2009 American Institute
for History Education

Teaching Suggestions

Activity I: Close Reading

1. Separate the class into pairs or trios and give each group a slip with an excerpt from *City Upon a Hill* (**Graphic Organizer A**). Have them put the sentence(s) in their own words. After a few moments, reconvene the class and distribute complete copies of **Handout A** to each student. Have groups read their paraphrases in turn, and discuss each as a class and decide if it is a faithful and complete paraphrase. Have students complete the chart on **Handout A** with the class paraphrases. When all slips are completed, read the original sermon aloud and discuss how the class version compared to the original.

2. On the back of each slip, have students identify the value(s) Winthrop encourages. Make a list of these values on the board, and discuss them as a large group.

- Are these the same kinds of values Americans should have today? Why or why not?

- Are there any values that are important today that Winthrop does not discuss?

- Are these uniquely American values, or are they broader than that?

Activity II: Creative Writing

1. Have students brainstorm other metaphors in *City Upon a Hill* that convey the meaning of America as an example or beacon for the world. *(e.g., a candle in the darkness; a lighthouse in the storm, etc.)* Keep a master list on the board, and discuss as a class the effectiveness of each. Then have each student select a metaphor to use in their own 10- to 12-sentence *City Upon a Hill* sermon. ("Sermons" should be titled using the new metaphor.)

Activity III: Application

1. Have students write a 6- to 8-sentence journal entry about a time they served as a role model or example to others. Entries should describe answers to the questions:

- In what way were you a role model?

- How did being a role model make you feel?

- How did your actions help someone else?

2. Then, ask students to imagine they are a young passenger aboard the *Arbella* and they are reflecting on Winthrop's sermon. Have them write a brief journal entry as that passenger, imagining what he or she was feeling and thinking as they sailed to their new settlement.

Activity IV: Synthesis

1. Distribute **Handout B** to all students. Read the Kennedy and Reagan speeches aloud (or give it to students who are strong readers to read aloud).

2. Tell students to divide a poster board into four quadrants. Label the first quadrant "Winthrop," the second one "Kennedy," the third one "Reagan," and put their names in the fourth quadrant. Using pencils, markers, photographs, or drawings, illustrate each quadrant with an American "city upon a hill" as the person imagined it.

Graphic Organizer A

The only way to avoid this shipwreck and to provide for our posterity is to do Justly, to love mercy, to walk humbly with our God	*Put this passage in your own words:*
We must be knit together in this work as one man, we must entertain each other in brotherly affection.	*Put this passage in your own words:*
Together in all meekness, gentleness, patience and liberality, we must delight in each other, mourn together, labor, and suffer together.	*Put this passage in your own words:*
Always having before our eyes … our community as members of the same body, so shall we keep the unity of the spirit in the bond of peace, the Lord will command a blessing upon us in all our ways.	*Put this passage in your own words:*
For we must consider that we shall be as a City Upon a Hill, the eyes of all people are upon us.	*Put this passage in your own words:*
So if we deal falsely with our God in this work we shall cause him to withdraw his present help from us. We shall be made a story through the world. If our hearts shall turn away, so that we will not obey, we shall surely perish out of the good land whither we pass over this vast sea to possess it.	*Put this passage in your own words:*
Therefore let us choose life, that we and our seed may live, by obeying His voice and cleaving to Him, for He is our life and our prosperity	*Put this passage in your own words:*

![American Institute for History Education logo]

Handout B

Ronald Reagan
In his 1989 Farewell Address, President Reagan said:

I've thought a bit of the shining "city upon a hill." The phrase comes from John Winthrop, who wrote it to describe the America he imagined. ... in my mind [America is] a tall proud city built on rocks stronger than oceans, wind-swept, God-blessed, and teeming with people of all kinds living in harmony and peace, a city with free ports that hummed with commerce and creativity, and if there had to be city walls, the walls had doors and the doors were open to anyone with the will and the heart to get here. That's how I saw it and see it still.

Ronald Reagan

John F. Kennedy
In a 1961 speech at the Massachusetts State House, President-elect Kennedy said:

I have been guided by the standard John Winthrop set before his shipmates on the flagship Arbella *331 years ago, as they, too, faced the task of building a new government on a perilous [dangerous] frontier. ... Today the eyes of all people are truly upon us — and our governments ... must be as a city upon a hill — constructed and inhabited by men aware of their great trust and their great responsibilities. Courage ... judgment ... integrity ... dedication ... these are the historic qualities of the Bay Colony and the Bay State [Massachusetts].*

John F. Kennedy

Thomas Paine's
Common Sense

fired the American heart in the Revolution, were pamphlets. Strike out of literature, ancient and modern, what
was first published in pamphlets, and you would leave it
the poorer and weaker to an incalculable degree.

Pamphlets and opinion,
and propag also store-
houses of fa biography,
records of g hronicles of
invention a row an un-
expected lig ll books are
silent. Bei n some sub-
ject that w en written,
they reflect cal, and re-
ligious spir h as news-
papers, they of it) of an
epoch, and at libraries
exhibit this spapers ex-
isted as veh the govern-
ment librari p for many
years past, of their re-
spective cou what, a cen-
tury ago, th ift.

When Th the s of
iver st in of
two centuri great
tector, he ollection of

pamphlets in the British se ary. An indefatig-
able patriot and bookseller, named Thoma had care-
fully gathered and kept

eared from the British press, during

Common Sense contains four sections. This abridged document begins with the original opening line of section III, which is entitled, "Thoughts on the Present State of American Affairs."

Notes: _____

_____

_____

_____

_____

_____

_____

_____

_____

_____

_____

_____

_____

_____

_____

_____

_____

_____

_____

_____

_____

_____

_____

Introduction

Thomas Paine

It was 1776, and the American colonists were growing tired of the British king's abuse. Some people thought the colonists should write letters, called petitions, to the king, telling him what they thought. They wanted the colonies to remain a part of England.

Other colonists believed that enough was enough. They had tried to work things out with the king, but it had not worked. They thought it was useless to try any longer. They believed that the colonies should declare independence from England.

Thomas Paine was one of the people who believed the colonies should be independent. He published **Common Sense** in 1776, hoping to convince others of his viewpoint. He succeeded. The Continental Congress declared independence from England just a few months after this pamphlet was published.

What Is a Primary Source?

A primary source is a piece of history. It is a document from a time period, like a diary, a speech, a newspaper article, or a photograph. In this chapter, you will study the pamphlet **Common Sense** as a primary source from 1776, as a way to learn about that time period of American history.

_____

_____

_____

_____

_____

Activating Prior Knowledge:
Questions for Pre-Reading Discussion

1. What do you know about the events that led the colonies to declare independence from England?

2. Have you ever heard of Thomas Paine? What do you know about him?

3. What do you think of when you hear the words "common sense"? Can you give examples of some things that are "common sense"?

4. Thomas Paine wanted to be independent of England. Have you ever wanted to make a permanent break from a group, club or team? What made you feel that way? How did you tell other participants?

Vocabulary and Context Questions

Using context clues and/or a dictionary, define each word:

Vocabulary

Plain: *clear and easily understood*

Cause: *effort, struggle*

Province: *a region of land*

Affair: *matter*

Reasonable: *sensible and logical*

Proper: *correct*

Absurd: *ridiculous*

Perpetually: *forever*

Independence: *freedom, being on one's own*

Context Questions

1. Who wrote this document? *Thomas Paine, a man who was born in England and came to America in 1774, wrote it.*

2. When did he write it? *1776*

3. What was his purpose? *To convince the colonists that it was time to declare independence from England*

4. Who read *Common Sense* (or whom did Paine want to read it)? *The American colonists read* Common Sense. *Paine also may have hoped that British citizens and officials would read his pamphlet.*

- Paine was born in England and came to the colonies after meeting Benjamin Franklin in London. Franklin, a well-respected American colonist, convinced Paine to come to America. He arrived in Philadelphia in 1774.

- *Common Sense* was first published on February 14, 1776.

- Most historians agree that at least 150,000 copies were printed, while some sources cite as many as 600,000 copies. *Common Sense* was the most widely read pamphlet of the Revolutionary era, outsold only by the Bible during its time.

- Paine used his own money to publish the first edition of *Common Sense*. He also donated all of his earnings from it to the Revolutionary cause.

- Despite his description of his argument as "common sense," Paine acknowledged in his introduction that he knew his ideas were not necessarily popular. Further, many believed the colonies should reconcile with England simply because that was the custom. *"A long habit of not thinking a thing wrong, gives it a superficial appearance of being right, and raises at first a formidable outcry in defense of custom. But tumult soon subsides. Time makes more converts than reason."*

Comprehension and Discussion Questions

- Why do you think Paine starts out with these lines? *To assure the reader that his argument will not be complicated. In fact, it will be "easy." Maybe that*

In the following pages I offer nothing more than simple facts, plain arguments, and common sense.

18

way people will be more likely to read it. Further, his argument is so "obvious" that he can state it very clearly.

- What does "common sense" mean to you? *Things everyone just "knows" because they are so apparent. Students may give examples from their pre-reading discussion, such as "look both ways before you cross the street," or, "check how deep the water is before you jump in," or "don't touch something on the stove."*

The Sun never shined on a cause of greater worth.
'Tis not the affair of a City, a County, a Province, or
a Kingdom; but of a Continent.

effort of a city or other small region, but of an entire continent.

- What do these lines seem designed to do? How do you think the colonists felt reading them? *They were probably meant to make the colonists feel empowered and important, especially compared with the small island (and Kingdom) of Britain.*

Notes: _____

_____

_____

_____

_____

_____

_____

_____

_____

_____

_____

_____

_____

_____

_____

_____

_____

_____

_____

_____

_____

19

Supplementary Information

- In the introduction to this work, Paine took this idea even further, saying that "The cause of America is, in a great measure, the cause of all mankind." That is, the colonies' struggle to be free of tyrannical government was a universal cause.

Comprehension and Discussion Questions

- How does Paine describe the cause of America? *As not the limited*

Supplementary Information

- In the years leading up to the publication of *Common Sense*, the colonists had experienced many violations of their rights by the British king. Property rights were not respected; accused persons were taken away to be tried by Admiralty Courts (by a judge with no jury); excessive fines and jail terms were imposed; and the king ignored the colonists' many petitions.

Comprehension and Discussion Questions

- What does Paine mean by "seed time"? *The time when something is planted, that will hopefully take root and grow. Paine hopes that this is what will happen with the cause of independence.*

- What does Paine want the colonists to have "faith" in? *In each other, and in what is right and just.*

Notes: _____

_____

_____

_____

_____

_____

_____

_____

_____

_____

_____

Now is the seed-time of Continental union, faith and honor.

20

_____

_____

_____

_____

But Britain is the parent country, say some ... but it happens not to be true, or only partly so ... Europe, and not England, is the parent country of America.

Supplementary Information

- Some Loyalists objected to independence on the grounds that England was the "mother country" and separation would be wrong.

- Enlightenment thinkers from France as well as England influenced many in the Revolutionary Era.

Comprehension and Discussion Questions

- Paine mentions the point of view that England is the "parent country" of America. Does Paine feel that way? *No, he does not believe that England is America's "parent country."*

- Who does Paine say is the parent country of America? *All of Europe.*

- Why do you think Paine believes this? *Colonists came to America from countries all over Europe, and not only from England. Not only that, but European philosophers were in some ways a "parent" to America in terms of giving life to the spirit of independence.*

Notes: _____

_____

_____

_____

_____

_____

_____

_____

_____

_____

_____

_____

_____

_____

_____

_____

_____

_____

Supplementary Information

- Thomas Paine was a believer in a philosophy known as natural law. Ancient Greek philosophers first identified a "natural" or universal law that existed everywhere and was distinct from customs or practices of a specific location. Natural law can be discovered through reason and moral principles. Natural law in practice will lead to human happiness.

- Paine and others believed that England's abuse of the colonists' rights was a violation of natural law.

- The battles of Lexington and Concord took place in April 1775, marking the beginning of the Revolutionary War.

Comprehension and Discussion Questions

- What does Paine say is "right and reasonable"? *Separation from England.*

- Paine talks about the "weeping voice of nature cries." What does he mean by "nature"? Does he mean "nature" like the outdoors: trees and plants, or does he mean something else? *Paine seems to use "nature" as a synonym for right or justice. Because nature is weeping; something has severely offended it.*

Notes: _____

_____

_____

_____

_____

Every thing that is right or reasonable pleads for separation. The blood of the slain, the weeping voice of nature cries, 'TIS TIME TO PART.

22

_____

_____

_____

_____

Small islands not capable of protecting themselves, are the proper objects for kingdoms to take under their care; but there is something very absurd, in supposing a continent to be perpetually governed by an island.

Supplementary Information

- Paine believes it is self-evident that Britain's perpetual rule of the colonies is wrong, in part because of their relative size and positions.

- In Section IV of *Common Sense*, Paine discusses the American military's capability: *"It is not in numbers, but in unity, that our great strength lies; yet our present numbers are sufficient to repel the force of all the world. The Continent hath, at this time, the largest body of armed and disciplined men of any power under Heaven."*

- George Washington was serving as Commander of the Continental Army as of June 1775.

Discussion and Comprehension Questions

- What kind of islands does Paine say a kingdom can rightly govern? *Small islands that are vulnerable because they cannot protect themselves.*

- What does this statement seem to say about America's ability to defend itself? *America can defend itself, it does not need England's protection.*

- What continent is Paine talking about? *America.*

- What island is Paine talking about? *England.*

- Why do you think Paine says it is "absurd" for a continent to be forever governed by an island? *The American colonies are much bigger than the island Great Britain. Put another way, America has "outgrown" the need for governance by the king.*

Notes: _____

_____

_____

_____

_____

_____

_____

_____

_____

_____

_____

Supplemental Information

- Self-government was considered by many enlightenment philosophers to be a natural right of humanity.

- Less than four months after *Common Sense* was published, the Continental Congress voted to declare independence from England.

- *Common Sense* was instrumental in swaying public opinion in support of independence.

- Although Paine played no part in framing the new United States government, he is considered by many to be a Founding Father because of his writings in *Common Sense* and other essays of the era, including *The American Crisis*.

- The Declaration of Independence, like *Common Sense*, also references natural (or unalienable) rights.

Comprehension and Discussion Questions

- What does Paine say is the only thing that will keep the peace? *Independence.*

- What kind of government does he call for? *A government of America's own.*

- What do you think he means by "our natural right"? *It makes sense that an independent society should have its own government. He believes that it is, as his title indicates, common sense.*

Notes: _____

_____

_____

Nothing but independence can keep the peace of the continent. A government of our own is our natural right.

24 _____

_____

_____

_____

_____

_____

Common Sense

In the following pages I offer nothing more than simple facts, plain arguments, and common sense.

The Sun never shined on a cause of greater worth. 'Tis not the affair of a City, a County, a Province, or a Kingdom; but of a Continent.

Now is the seed-time of Continental union, faith and honor.

But Britain is the parent country, say some. But it happens not to be true, or only partly so. Europe, and not England, is the parent country of America.

Every thing that is right or reasonable pleads for separation. The blood of the slain, the weeping voice of nature cries, 'TIS TIME TO PART.

Small islands not capable of protecting themselves, are the proper objects for kingdoms to take under their care; but there is something very absurd, in supposing a continent to be perpetually governed by an island.

Nothing but independence can keep the peace of the continent. A government of our own is our natural right.

Wrap-up Discussion Questions

- How do you think the colonists felt when they read *Common Sense*?

- If you had to explain to someone what Thomas Paine says in *Common Sense* using only one sentence, what would it be?

- Why do you think Paine titled his pamphlet *Common Sense*?

- What seems most important to Thomas Paine?

- How do you think the British king would have reacted to this pamphlet?

- Thomas Paine did not play a role in creating the new United States government. But his writings influenced many to support independence. Should he be known as a Founding Father?

- Why do you think Americans remember this pamphlet more than 200 years later?

- Thomas Paine had a message he wanted to bring to a large audience. What kinds of ways do you have today to tell others what you believe?

American Institute
FOR HISTORY EDUCATION
"Well done is better than well said"

© 2009 American Institute
for History Education

Teaching Suggestions

Activity I: Close Reading

Separate the class into pairs or trios and give each group a slip with an excerpt from *Common Sense* (**Graphic Organizer A**). Have them put the sentence(s) in their own words. After a few moments, reconvene the class and distribute complete copies of **Handout A** to each student. Have groups read their paraphrases in turn, and discuss each as a class and decide if it is a faithful and complete paraphrase. Have students complete the chart on **Handout A** with the class paraphrases. When all slips are completed, read the original version of *Common Sense* aloud and discuss how the class version compared with the original.

Activity II: Compare and Contrast

Explain to students that Paine and others have been called the "Bloggers of the Revolution." Have students brainstorm all the ways people today have to communicate their ideas to others (*e.g., writing in newspapers, speaking on television, e-mail, text-messaging, Internet blogs, etc.*) Then ask them to consider what methods Paine could use during the American Revolution to have his voice heard. Have them make a T-chart with one side labeled "Ways to communicate in 1776," and the other "Ways I can communicate today." For each method, have students estimate the time needed for that communication to take place.

Activity III: Creative Writing

1. Ask students to imagine they are trying to convince other people about something that is important to them. Have them work in groups to brainstorm initial ideas for topics. Then have them write a 10-line "pamphlet" in the style of Paine, in which they offer "plain facts and common sense" in support of their viewpoint.

2. Have students imagine they have been hired by a Thomas Paine historical society to create a modern web site for people who want to learn about him and about *Common Sense*. Using markers and/or magazine cutouts, have students create a home page for Thomas Paine. Pages should be titled and include at least three descriptive sentences and three images. (See **Handout B: Web site Template** for ideas)

   (*Alternate:* Ask students to assume the persona of Thomas Paine and create a blog or MySpace page. What would Paine's screen name be? Who would he put on his "Friends" list? What picture would he use for an avatar? What kinds of images would he put on his page? Use **Handout B: Web site Template** for ideas.)

Activity IV: Application

Ask students to imagine they are young American colonists who have read *Common Sense* and have been persuaded to support independence. Imagining that the Internet existed in 1776, have them compose a two- to three-entry blog in which they explain why they support breaking from England. Students should remember that their friends back in England will be able to read their blogs.

Graphic Organizer A

In the following pages I offer nothing more than simple facts, plain arguments, and common sense.	*Put this passage in your own words:*
The Sun never shined on a cause of greater worth. 'Tis not the affair of a City, a County, a Province, or a Kingdom; but of a Continent.	*Put this passage in your own words:*
Now is the seed-time of Continental union, faith and honor.	*Put this passage in your own words:*
But Britain is the parent country, say some. But it happens not to be true, or only partly so. Europe, and not England, is the parent country of America.	*Put this passage in your own words:*
Every thing that is right or reasonable pleads for separation. The blood of the slain, the weeping voice of nature cries, 'TIS TIME TO PART.	*Put this passage in your own words:*
Small islands not capable of protecting themselves, are the proper objects for kingdoms to take under their care; but there is something very absurd, in supposing a continent to be perpetually governed by an island.	*Put this passage in your own words:*
Nothing but independence can keep the peace of the continent. A government of our own is our natural right.	*Put this passage in your own words:*

Name: _____ **Date:** _____

Handout B: Web site Template

Web site Title: www. _____ .org

Picture	*Picture*

Interesting Information:

Picture

The Declaration of Independence

When in the Course of human events it becomes necessary for one people

them with another and to assume among the powers of the earth. the sep

nd of Nature's 𝒢   the opinions of ma

impel them to the   o be self evident.

that all men are 𝑒   y their Creator w

certain unalienab   liberty. and the

pursuit of happine   nments are institu

amoung men. der   nt of the governed

That whenever an   ctive of thses ends

it is the right of t   d institute new go

laying its foundat   ng its powers in su

form as to them sh   fety and happines

Prudence. indeed   established should

not be changed fo.   ordingly all exper

hath shown that m   while evils are suf

than to right them   ch they are accusto

But when a long   suing invariably

the same object evinces a design to reduce t'em under absolute despotism.

it is their right. it is their duty . . . ow off such government. and . . p

new gaurds . . . r futur security . . . been the . . . tient sufferance

of ther . . . . hem to

. . . . Kin

. . . . al

This abridged version of the Declaration of Independence begins with the second paragraph of the Declaration. The first paragraph, the Preamble, reads: *"When in the Course of human events it becomes necessary for one people to dissolve the political bands which have connected them with another and to assume among the powers of the earth, the separate and equal station to which the Laws of Nature and of Nature's God entitle them, a decent respect to the opinions of mankind requires that they should declare the causes which impel them to the separation.*

Notes: _____

_____

_____

_____

_____

_____

_____

_____

_____

_____

_____

_____

_____

_____

_____

_____

Introduction

As British citizens, the colonists believed they had certain rights the king was supposed to respect. These rights were called "the rights of Englishmen." But the king had been abusing his power and violating the colonists' rights. He had taken their property, taxed them unfairly, forced them to let British troops stay in their homes, and many other unfair things. They tried for many years to convince the king to stop. But he did not.

Thomas Jefferson

In 1776, the colonists decided to declare independence from England and form a new government for themselves. This new government would be very different from the government in England. In England, a king took the throne and ruled by birth. The United States government, on the other hand, would be created by the people.

The colonists would base their country on the idea that all people were born with certain rights. These rights were given to them by their Creator. At this time, many colonists owned slaves. Women and other groups were denied many legal rights. However, the ideals of the Declaration of Independence, written mostly by Thomas Jefferson, have been called upon through American history in the name of extending the blessings of liberty to all.

What Is a Primary Source?

A primary source is a piece of history. It is a document from a time period, like a diary, a speech, a newspaper article, or a photograph.

In this chapter you will study the **Declaration of Independence** as a primary source from 1776, as a way to learn about that time period of American history.

_____

_____

_____

_____

_____

Activating Prior Knowledge:
Questions for Pre-Reading Discussion

1. The United States started out as colonies of another country. Do you know which country?

2. Do you know why the United States declared independence?

3. Why do we celebrate Independence Day? Does your family have any special Fourth of July activities or traditions?

4. What are "rights"? Are there rights you think all people have — or should have?

5. Did you know that important people from history, including Elizabeth Cady Stanton, Abraham Lincoln and Martin Luther King Jr. all quoted the Declaration of Independence? Why do you think they did this?

6. Have you ever wanted to declare your independence from something?

Vocabulary and Context Questions

Using context clues and/or a dictionary, define each word:

Vocabulary

Self-evident: *clear, easily understood without explanation*

Endowed: *awarded or given*

Unalienable rights: *rights everyone is born with, and which cannot justly be taken away without consent*

Pursuit: *hunt, chase, or quest for*

Secure: *make safe*

Instituted: *formed or established*

Deriving: *getting*

Consent: *permission*

Destructive: *hurtful to*

Ends: *purposes*

Abolish: *get rid of*

Effect: *bring about*

Solemnly: *seriously, formally*

Providence: *the protection of their God, destiny, fate*

Context Questions

1. Who wrote this document? *Thomas Jefferson, on behalf of the Continental Congress*

2. When did he write this document? *1776*

3. What was his purpose? *To declare independence from England for the United States, and to explain the philosophy behind the separation*

4. Who is the audience for this document? *The people of the United States, and the king of England*

Supplementary Information

- Thomas Jefferson was one of a "Committee of Five" chosen to write the Declaration. Jefferson asked John Adams and Benjamin Franklin to read his draft and offer advice on improving it.

- One of Jefferson's key influences in drafting the Declaration was English philosopher John Locke's *Two Treatises of Civil Government*, published in 1690.

- John Locke stated that all men were "equal and independent."

- These opening lines are similar to the Virginia Declaration of Rights, written by fellow Virginian George Mason and issued on June 12, 1776: "all men are by nature equally free and independent ... "

- The Founding Fathers believed that rights did not belong only to Englishmen. They asserted that all people were born with the same rights, regardless of what country they were from. Many of the colonists owned slaves, and this was in contradiction to this belief. However, many of them hoped and worked for the abolition of slavery.

- Abraham Lincoln quoted these words in the 1863 Gettysburg Address, when he said the United States must abolish slavery to live up to its ideals.

Comprehension and Discussion Questions

- What do think "all men are created equal" means? *All people are equal when they are conceived or when they are born, or, all people naturally have equal rights.*

- Many of the colonists owned slaves, including the author of

We hold these truths to be self-evident, that all men are created equal,

the Declaration of Independence, Thomas Jefferson. Does that seem to go against what they wrote here? Why did they write it, then? *Answers will vary. It is a contradiction that the colonists contended for their own liberty while denying liberty to Africans. Some students may say that many in the Founding generation knew this, and worked to bring about the abolition of slavery.*

- Did women have the same legal rights as men when the Declaration of Independence was written? Do they now? *They did not in 1776; they do now.*

that they are endowed by their Creator with certain unalienable rights,

Supplementary Information

- John Locke used the term "inalienable rights."

- These lines are also similar to the Virginia Declaration of Rights, which reads: "That all men ... have certain inherent rights."

- This passage refers to man's "Creator." In other places, the Declaration refers to "the laws of nature and nature's God" and the protection of "divine Providence."

- The Declaration of Independence is not a source of law. Rather, it is a statement of political philosophy.

Comprehension and Discussion Questions

- According to the Declaration, who gives people their rights? *Their Creator. In other words, all people are born with these rights, including slaves, women, and American Indians.*

- "Unalienable" rights cannot be taken away. What are some things you think people have a right to do? *Answers will vary, but students may suggest they have the right to make choices about their life, to say what they believe, to choose their own religion, to travel.*

- Do you believe children have the same inalienable rights as adults? Do you have the same rights as your parents? *Answers will vary.*

Notes: _____

_____

_____

_____

_____

_____

_____

_____

_____

_____

_____

_____

_____

_____

Supplementary Information

- John Locke stated that natural rights included "life, liberty" and "estate" or "property."

- Again, these lines mirror the text of the Virginia Declaration of Rights, which reads: "namely, the enjoyment of life and liberty, with the means of acquiring and possessing property, and pursuing and obtaining happiness and safety."

- According to the Fifth Amendment, ratified in 1791, no person shall be deprived of "life, liberty, or property" without due process of law. In this way, individuals' life, liberty and property were legally protected from unreasonable action by government.

Comprehension and Discussion Questions

- What do you think of when you hear the word "liberty"? *Freedom, being able to do what you like, making choices, being free of unjust restraint.*

- What does the word "pursuit" mean to you? *To pursue something is to try to catch it.*

- How do you pursue happiness? *Students may suggest being with family and friends, doing hobbies they enjoy, practicing their religion, doing a good job on things that are important to them, succeeding in school, etc.*

- Why do you think Jefferson said "pursuit of happiness" and not just "happiness"? *Answers will vary. Some students may suggest a right to happiness would be impossible. Others may say this means if you are not happy, you*

that among these are life, liberty and the pursuit of happiness.

32

can keep trying different things until you find something that makes you happy.

Notes: _____

_____

_____

_____

That to secure these rights, governments are instituted among men, deriving their just powers from the consent of the governed,

Supplementary Information

- John Locke stated, "The liberty of man, in society, is to be under no other legislative power, but that established, by consent, in the commonwealth. ... Men being, as has been said, by nature, all free, equal, and independent, no one can be ... subjected to the political power of another, without his own consent."

- The Virginia Declaration of Rights states: "That all power is vested in, and consequently derived from, the people."

- The Founders studied Ancient Republics, and the writings of British and French philosophers, including Locke and Baron de Montesquieu. Based on these studies, they concluded that a representative democracy, or republic, was best suited to human happiness.

- The principle that just government power comes from the people is called "popular sovereignty."

Comprehension and Discussion Questions

- According to the Declaration of Independence, where does government get its power from? "The consent of the governed," in other words, from the permission of the people.

- Do you know how this idea is different from how a king or queen gets their power? Or a dictator? *Kings or queens rule by heredity (because their parent or other close family members was a king or queen), or by claimed divine right. Dictators come to power by overthrowing a current government by force.*

- Which kind of community would you rather live in? Why? *Students will probably say they prefer to live in a society where officials have the consent of the people to govern.*

- What are ways people in the United States give their "consent" to government? *By voting, by writing letters and telling government what they think, by having the option to impeach leaders, by choosing to live here — citizens are free to leave, and live elsewhere unlike in totalitarian societies where no one is allowed to leave.*

Supplementary Information

- John Locke stated, "The end of government is the good of mankind." He also believed that the most important inalienable right was political judgment — including the right to abolish a tyrannical government.

- The Virginia Declaration of Rights stated, "whenever any government shall be found inadequate or contrary to these purposes, a majority of the community hath an indubitable, unalienable, and indefeasible right to reform, alter or abolish it, in such manner as shall be judged most conducive to the public weal."

- In other sections of the Declaration, Jefferson cautions that long-established governments should not be done away with for light and temporary reasons. Rather, it is only after a "long train of abuses" that abolishing government is justified. The Declaration presents a long list of grievances against the king, explaining how he has abused his power.

Comprehension and Discussion Questions

- What does the Declaration say people have the right to do whenever a form of government fails to protect peoples' inalienable rights? *To "alter or abolish" it — that is, to change it or get rid of it altogether. (They then have the right to form a new, better government.)*

- Does this sound like a really new and even scary idea to you? *Probably not.*

- How do you think it sounded to

that whenever any form of government becomes destructive of these ends, it is the right of the people to alter or to abolish it, and to institute new government, ... in such form, as to them shall seem most likely to effect their safety and happiness.

34

the king of England? *Students may recognize how radical an idea this was, and how it was truly defying the king's power.*

Notes: _____

_____

_____

_____

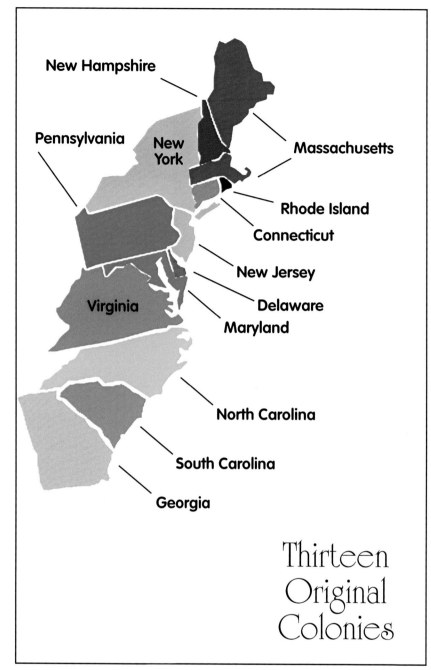

We, therefore, ... solemnly publish and declare, that these united colonies are, and of right ought to be, free and independent states.

Supplementary Information

- The Declaration was not addressed to the king, but rather to "a candid world."

- The Lee Resolution was introduced in the Continental Congress by Richard Henry Lee of Virginia on June 7, 1776. It read, *"Resolved, That these United Colonies are, and of right ought to be, free and independent States, that they are absolved from all allegiance to the British Crown, and that all political connection between them and the*

State of Great Britain is, and ought to be, totally dissolved."

- Congress voted to declare independence from England on July 2, 1776.

- The final wording of the Declaration of Independence was approved by Congress on July 4, 1776.

- Some Founding Fathers believed that the United States would celebrate Independence Day on July 2, not July 4.

- As president of the Continental Congress, John Hancock was the only person to sign the Declaration on July 4, 1776. He did not sign it in front of a room full of people, as is often shown in paintings. Rather, it is likely that the only other person present was the secretary of Congress, Charles Thomson. The rest of the delegates did not sign the declaration until August.

Comprehension and Discussion Questions

- What is being stated in these lines of the Declaration? *This portion actually declares independence from England.*

- How do you think the colonists felt about these lines? *Bold, happy, resolved, defiant, proud, excited, or perhaps scared of what might happen in the future.*

Notes: _____

_____

_____

_____

_____

Supplemental Information

- Fifty-six men signed the Declaration. These included two future presidents: John Adams and Thomas Jefferson. The youngest signer, Edward Rutledge, was 26. Ben Franklin was the oldest signer, at age 70.

- The last surviving signer of the Declaration was Charles Carroll of Carrollton, Maryland. He died in 1832, at the age of 96.

- A Philadelphia printer, John Dunlap, printed at least 200 "broadsides" of the Declaration to be distributed.

- One of these broadsides, produced the night of July 4, 1776, is on display at the National Archives in Washington, D.C.

- In 1989, a man bought a painting at a flea market because he liked the frame it was in. He paid $4 for it. Later, he discovered that hidden in the backing of the frame was an Original Dunlap Broadside of the Declaration of Independence. It sold two years later at a New York City auction for $8.14 million.

Comprehension and Discussion Questions

- What did the signers of the Declaration say they would rely on for the support of the Declaration? *Divine providence, as well as each other.*

- Why do you think they added this last line? *To show they were united and all devoted to the cause of independence; they were aware of the possible penalties for defying the king.*

And for the support of this declaration, with a firm reliance on the protection of Divine Providence, we mutually pledge to each other our lives, our fortunes, and our sacred honor.

36

- What is your "sacred honor"? *Your word, or your integrity.*

- How do you act in honorable ways in your own life? *Answers will vary, but students should note being honest, keeping promises, standing up for one's beliefs, defending ideals.*

Notes: _____

_____

_____

Declaration
of Independence

We hold these truths to be self-evident,
that all men are created equal,

that they are endowed by their Creator
with certain unalienable rights,

that among these are life, liberty
and the pursuit of happiness.

That to secure these rights, governments are
instituted among men, deriving their just powers
from the consent of the governed,

that whenever any form of government becomes
destructive of these ends, it is the right of the
people to alter or to abolish it, and to institute new
government, ... in such form, as to them shall seem
most likely to effect their safety and happiness.

We, therefore, ... solemnly publish and declare,
that these united colonies are, and of right
ought to be, free and independent states.

And for the support of this declaration, with a
firm reliance on the protection of Divine Providence,
we mutually pledge to each other our lives,
our fortunes, and our sacred honor.

Name: _____ **Date:** _____

Wrap-up Discussion Questions

- The colonists knew that the king would consider declaring independence from England to be an act of treason. Why did they still decide to do it?

- Do you think it took courage for the delegates to vote to declare independence, and to sign their names to this document?

- The Declaration of Independence has been called "American Scripture." (Scripture usually means writing that is holy.) Why do you think it is called that?

- How would you explain what the Declaration of Independence says if a friend asked you?

- Is the Declaration still important today, more than 200 years after it was written?

Teaching Suggestions

Activity I: Close Reading

Separate the class into pairs or trios and give each group a slip of paper with an excerpt from the Declaration of Independence (**Graphic Organizer A**). Have them put the phrase(s) in their own words. After a few moments, reconvene the class and distribute complete copies of **Handout A** to each student. Have groups read their paraphrases in turn, and discuss each as a class and decide if it is a faithful and complete paraphrase. Have students complete the chart on **Handout A** with the class paraphrases. When all slips are completed, read the Declaration aloud and discuss how the class version compared with the original.

Activity II: Additional Primary Sources

Distribute **Handout B: Quotes on the Declaration** and have students select one quotation for which to write a three- to four-sentence response. Conduct a large group discussion where students share their responses, and discuss further the ideas behind them.

Activity III: Creative Storytelling

The original Declaration signed by Hancock and Thomson on July 4, 1776, has been lost. Have students imagine what might have happened to it, and write a short story, graphic novel, or play describing the fictional events. They should include "characters" from the era (*e.g., Thomas Jefferson, John Hancock, John Adams, Benjamin Franklin, and/or others*).

Activity IV: Extensions

Have students visit the web site **www.archives.gov/national-archives-experience/charters/declaration.html** and view images of the Declaration of Independence. Then discuss as a class:

- Is the Declaration hard to read? Why?

- Before the days of television and the Internet, how do you think people learned about the Declaration?

- How long do you think it took for news of the Declaration to reach all of the colonies? The king of England?

Graphic Organizer A

We hold these truths to be self-evident, that all men are created equal,	*Put this passage in your own words:*
that they are endowed by their Creator with certain unalienable rights,	*Put this passage in your own words:*
that among these are life, liberty and the pursuit of happiness.	*Put this passage in your own words:*
That to secure these rights, governments are instituted among men, deriving their just powers from the consent of the governed.	*Put this passage in your own words:*
That whenever any form of government becomes destructive of these ends, it is the right of the people to alter or to abolish it, and to institute new government, in such form, as to them shall seem most likely to effect their safety and happiness.	*Put this passage in your own words:*
We, therefore, solemnly publish and declare, That these united colonies are, and of right ought to be free and independent states.	*Put this passage in your own words:*
And for the support of this Declaration, with a firm reliance on the protection of Divine Providence, we mutually pledge to each other our lives, our fortunes and our sacred honor.	*Put this passage in your own words:*

Handout B: Quotes on the Declaration

Directions: Choose one quotation and write a three- to four-sentence response.

The second day of July 1776 will be the most memorable [day], in the history of America.
... It ought to be solemnized with games, sports, guns, bells, [and] bonfires
... from one end of this continent to the other from this time forward forever more.
— John Adams

We must all hang together, or most assuredly, we will all hang separately.
— Benjamin Franklin

The object of the Declaration of Independence [was] to place before mankind
the common sense of the subject.
— Thomas Jefferson

Here, Sir, the people govern.
— Alexander Hamilton

To contend for our liberty, and to deny that blessing to others,
involves an inconsistency not to be excused.
— John Jay

Preamble
to the
Constitution

We the People of the States United to form a more perfect Union, establish Justice, insure domestic Tran-quility, provide for the common defense, promote the general Welfare, and secure the Blessings of Liberty to ourselves and our Posterity

The Preamble to the Constitution is reproduced here in its entirety.

Notes: _____

_____

_____

_____

_____

_____

_____

_____

_____

_____

_____

_____

_____

_____

_____

_____

_____

_____

_____

_____

_____

_____

Introduction

The United States declared its independence from England in 1776. The Revolutionary War was fought for freedom and liberty. In 1781, the states came together under the Articles of Confederation. But many soon saw that the Articles of Confederation did not give America the kind of government it needed.

Gouverneur Morris

During the summer of 1787, fifty-five men from twelve of the thirteen states met in Philadelphia to write a new constitution for the United States. This meeting was called the Constitutional Convention, and the people who attended were called delegates.

The delegates picked a committee to take the Convention's ideas and write the final Constitution. One member of that committee was named Gouverneur (Goo-vun-eer) Morris. Morris was chosen to write an introduction to the Constitution. That introduction is called the Preamble. It explains the purposes of the national government.

What Is a Primary Source?

A primary source is a piece of history. It is a document from a time period, like a diary, a speech, a newspaper article, or a photograph. In this chapter, you will study the **Preamble** as a primary source from 1787, as a way to learn about that time period of American history.

40

_____

_____

_____

_____

Activating Prior Knowledge:
Questions for Pre-Reading Discussion

1. What do you know about the United States Constitution?

2. Do you know how our form of government is different from a monarchy? How is the American president different from a king or queen?

3. Have you ever heard the phrase "We the people"? What does it mean to you?

4. What kinds of things do you believe government should do for the nation? What kinds of rules and laws are needed?

5. The Constitution was created by more than fifty people from a dozen states. Do you ever work together with different kinds of people? How do you find things in common?

6. The people who wrote the Constitution said they wanted to make sure the people who came after them could live in liberty. Do you ever do things for people in the future? Why?

Vocabulary and Context Questions

Complete this page as you read. Using context clues and/or a dictionary, define each word:

Vocabulary

Establish: *create a foundation for*

Justice: *a fair system of laws*

Domestic: *within the country*

Tranquility: *serenity, peace*

Defense: *a nation's security against attack*

Promote: *to make better*

Welfare: *best interest, happiness*

Liberty: *freedom to act without unauthorized restraint*

Posterity: *future generations*

Ordain: *proclaim*

Context Questions

1. Who wrote this document? *Gouverneur Morris, on behalf of the delegates to the Constitutional Convention*

2. When did he write this document? *1787*

3. What was his purpose? *To write an introduction to the new plan of government created by the Convention*

4. Who is the audience for this document? *The people of the United States of America — in 1787, today, and in the future*

Supplementary Information

- Gouverneur Morris, the Preamble's author, was born in New York. He moved to Philadelphia in 1779 and represented Pennsylvania at the Convention.

- Morris's leg had been injured in a carriage accident and had to be amputated below the knee. He had a wooden leg.

- Morris had the reputation for being a "rake" or a ladies' man. He married at age 57. With this marriage, he became related to Thomas Jefferson.

- The phrase "We the People" was very controversial during the ratification debates. Some argued that the Constitution should begin with the phrase "We the states."

- The Constitution was sent to the states for ratification (approval) in 1787. Delaware was the first state to ratify it, on December 7, 1787.

- New Hampshire was the ninth state to ratify the Constitution, on June 21, 1788. Once it did, the Constitution became the law of the land for those nine states.

- The remaining states had all ratified the Constitution by May 1790.

Comprehension and Discussion Questions

- According to the Preamble, who wrote the Constitution, and for whom? *The people of the United States.*

- At the time of the Constitution, most rulers on Earth were dictators or kings. Why was the United States Constitution so different? *The government of the United States would get its power from the people. Officials would govern*

We the people of the United States,

42

not by force, by birth, or by claimed divine right, but by the consent of the governed.

- Were all the people of the United States included in this phrase? *Answers will vary. The Founding Fathers believed that all people were born with an equality of natural rights. Women and slaves, however, were not allowed to take part in the political process and were denied many civil and political rights. Some will say that the phrase included all people in theory, despite this difference in protected rights. Others will say it only included citizens, or voting citizens.*

in order to form a more perfect Union,

Supplementary Information

- In the 1780s, many people saw problems with the Articles of Confederation. The initial plan was to revise the Articles. It was soon decided, however, to start over with a new plan of government.

- The Articles referred to the states as in "perpetual union." By contrast, the Preamble declares its intention to form a "more perfect union."

Comprehension and Discussion Questions

- Why do you think the Preamble says "a more perfect union"? *"More perfect" than what? Than the union under the Articles of Confederation.*

- Do you ever try to improve on things you've done? Name some of those examples. *Students may say they try to improve on their schoolwork, or in sports, or in the development of individual talents like artwork, music, dance, chess, or other activities.*

- Have you ever made a plan at school or with your family, and then part of the way into it decided you needed to change the plan, or even start over? How did you handle that? *Answers will vary.*

Notes: _____

_____

_____

_____

_____

_____

_____

_____

_____

_____

_____

_____

_____

_____

_____

_____

Supplementary Information

- This is the first purpose of the new plan of government explained by the Preamble. The Preamble just puts in plain words what the Constitution will do; it is *not* a source of federal government power.

- The Constitution places limits on suspension of *habeas corpus* and provides for jury trials in all criminal cases. The Bill of Rights, ratified in 1791, provides additional protections for due process of law and freedom from unreasonable government action.

- The Constitution also defines treason and explains how it can be proved.

Comprehension and Discussion Questions

- What does the word "justice" mean to you? *Answers will vary. Students may suggest laws that apply to everybody the same, punishments for crimes, rules for the police and for the court system.*

- Is there more than one kind of justice? If so, what kinds of justice are there? *Students may suggest civil justice, criminal justice, and fair treatment.*

- Can you think of examples of justice in school or in your family? *School codes of conduct, fair treatment and equal punishments for the same wrongdoings; it can also mean treating people differently: giving students who need it more help in math, for example, may be a just action, even though it means the kids who do not need the extra help do not receive it.*

establish justice,

44

- Of all these kinds of justice, which do you think the Constitution was establishing? *Criminal and civil justice. The Constitution only limits government action.*

Notes: _____

_____

_____

insure domestic tranquility,

Comprehension and Discussion Questions

- What does "domestic" mean? *In the United States.*

- Tranquility means peace or serenity. What kinds of places or experiences can you think of that are tranquil? *Answers will vary. Students may suggest relaxing at home, going camping with family, playing games they enjoy, or other peaceful and serene activities.*

- What do you think might be the opposite of tranquility? *Stress, fighting, unrest, turmoil, disorder, war.*

- Why do you think Morris chose this word? *To express that a key purpose of government was to make sure there was peace at home.*

Notes: _____

_____

_____

_____

_____

_____

_____

_____

_____

_____

_____

_____

_____

_____

_____

_____

Supplementary Information

- The new plan of government had to address both domestic and international concerns. "Domestic" tranquility means tranquility at home in the United States.

- The Constitution guarantees each state a republican form of government, and forbids states from doing things like coining their own money or making treaties — these partly ensure that the Union will be peaceable.

Supplementary Information

- Congress is given the express power to provide for the common defense and to raise an army and navy in Article I, Section 8.

- Article I gives Congress the power to declare war, and Article II gives the president the power to act as commander in chief of the military.

Comprehension and Discussion Questions

- What does "the common defense" mean? *The ability of the country to defend itself from attack.*

- What are examples of America's national defense? *The armed services: the Army, Navy, Air Force, Marine Corps, and Coast Guard, defend the United States in times of attack or war. Further, government officers who take part in shaping the country's foreign policy include Cabinet members who advise the president on national security, and others.*

Notes: _____

_____

_____

_____

_____

_____

_____

_____

_____

_____

provide for the common defense,

_____

_____

_____

_____

_____

promote the general welfare,

Supplementary Information

- The phrase "general welfare" appeared in the Articles of Confederation: "The said States hereby severally enter into a firm league of friendship with each other, for their common defense, the security of their liberties, and their mutual and general welfare ... "

- Article I, Section 8, gives Congress the power to "provide for the common Defense and general Welfare of the United States."

- The general welfare clause of Article I, Section 8, was one of the most controversial during the ratification debate. Some believed it was too broad a grant of power, and could be used to justify any almost kind of federal law that Congress claimed was in the country's best interest.

- The term "welfare" was not, in this context, used to refer to public assistance to the needy as it is used commonly to mean today.

Comprehension and Discussion Questions

- The phrase "general welfare" shows that the government represents all people equally. Is that an important quality of our government? *Students should recognize that the Constitution set up a government that would treat the interests of all persons equally.*

- What would happen if leaders favored one group of people? *Things would not be fair; some people would have unfair advantages; it would be like the government "playing favorites."*

- What kinds of things can you think of that are part of the country's "general welfare?" *Peace among the states, peace within individual states, the right of citizens to travel, and others.*

Notes: _____

_____

_____

_____

_____

_____

47

Supplemental Information

- "Liberty" means freedom from unauthorized restraint. The Founding Fathers considered liberty to be an inalienable right of all people.

- They believed that the blessings of liberty were included.

- The Constitution was signed on September 17, 1787, at the Philadelphia State House in Pennsylvania. It was then sent to the states for ratification. It would not be truly "established" as the law of the land until nine states had ratified it. It would then take effect for those states.

- The ratification of the Constitution was not assured. A debate emerged between Federalists, who supported the Constitution, and Anti-Federalists, who did not.

- The most famous defense of the Constitution was *The Federalist* papers. This series of essays was written by Alexander Hamilton, John Jay, and James Madison.

- The Constitution has been in force longer than any other written constitution in the world.

Comprehension and Discussion Questions

- The Founding Fathers talked and wrote a lot about liberty. Why do you think it was so important to them? *Answers will vary. Students may say it was because they wanted to be free to do what they wanted, as long as they did not hurt others. Some students may point out that they had recently thrown off oppressive government, and were more concerned with liberty.*

and secure the blessings of liberty to ourselves and our posterity, do ordain and establish this Constitution for the United States of America.

- What group of people had no liberty during the time of the Constitution? *Slaves. Slaves were people but were treated as property. The Thirteenth Amendment to the Constitution, passed in 1865, outlawed slavery in the United States.*

- Who is "our posterity" in this statement? *Future generations. Their children, and their children's children.*

- How much liberty do you have in your life now? How much will you have when you are 12? When you are 18? *Answers will vary, but*

Note to teacher: This page does not appear in the student version of *Documents for Democracy*.

students should note that liberty will increase with age. You may point out that this additional liberty will be because of the corresponding increase in responsibility.

- What are some "blessings of liberty" in your life? *Answers will vary, but students may suggest being able to make choices about things that are important to them, like reading books they like, playing sports they enjoy, being able to be with their families, being able to travel, etc.*

- Ministers and clergy are sometimes called "ordained." What does the

word sound like it means? *To make something sacred or very special.*

- The people established the Constitution for what? *The United States of America.*

- The introduction to the Constitution is 52 words. Would it have been better if it were shorter? Or if it were longer? Or is it just right? *Answers will vary.*

Notes: _____

_____

_____

_____

_____

_____

_____

_____

_____

_____

_____

_____

_____

_____

_____

_____

_____

_____

_____

_____

_____

Preamble to the Constitution

We the people of the United States,

in order to form a more perfect Union,

establish justice,

insure domestic tranquility,

provide for the common defense,

promote the general welfare,

and secure the blessings of liberty to ourselves and our posterity, do ordain and establish this Constitution for the United States of America.

Wrap-up Discussion Questions

- Perseverance means to keep trying, even if it means having to work very hard to overcome things. Was the Constitutional Convention an example of perseverance for the new nation? Why or why not?

- In what ways have you shown perseverance in your own life?

- The Preamble was written as an introduction to the Constitution. Was it an important job to write the Preamble? How do you think Gouverneur Morris felt about it?

- The Preamble lists six general purposes of the national government. How would you describe these purposes?

Teaching Suggestions

Activity I: Close Reading

Separate the class into pairs or trios and give each group a slip of paper with an excerpt from the Preamble (**Graphic Organizer A**). Have them put the phrase(s) in their own words. After a few moments, reconvene the class and distribute complete copies of **Handout A** to each student. Have groups read their paraphrases in turn, and discuss each as a class and decide if it is a faithful and complete paraphrase. Have students complete the chart on **Handout A** with the class paraphrases. When all slips are completed, read the Preamble aloud and discuss how the class version compared to the original.

Activity II: Creative Writing

Ask students to imagine they are writing a letter to a friend in another country. Their friend has never been to America and doesn't understand what the national government does. Using what they learned by reading the Preamble, have students explain the purposes of the national government to their friend in a one-page letter.

Activity III: Application

1. Put students in groups of six. Give each group a piece of butcher paper or poster board with a large hexagon drawn on it. Have students label each of the six sides with one purpose of the government listed in the Preamble.

2. Assign one group member to each purpose, *(e.g., one student would work on "form a more perfect union," another on "establish justice," and so on.)*

3. Have students work on their own paper to draw a symbol or illustration of that government purpose. You also may wish to give them newspapers or magazines to cut out pictures for a collage.

4. When all group members have finished, have groups come to the front of the room and have each student explain his or her contribution to the project. Display all the posters around the room and allow students to view them all.

Activity IV: Extensions

1. Have students work in pairs to list and discuss their favorite things to do each day. Then, using **Handout B: How Much Liberty?**, have them shade in the line under each activity showing how much liberty they have while doing it. They should write a one- or two-sentence explanation.

2. Reconvene the class and ask students to share the types of actions they listed. Discuss the following questions:

   - Did their favorite activities allow them to have liberty?

   - Is there a connection between happiness and liberty?

   - What is the opposite of liberty?

   - Is respecting other peoples' liberty important?

   - Returning again to the Preamble, why do you think the Founding Fathers wanted their new government to protect liberty?

Name: _____ **Date:** _____

Graphic Organizer A

We the people of the United States,	*Put this passage in your own words:*
in order to form a more perfect union,	*Put this passage in your own words:*
establish justice,	*Put this passage in your own words:*
insure domestic tranquility,	*Put this passage in your own words:*
provide for the common defense,	*Put this passage in your own words:*
promote the general welfare,	*Put this passage in your own words:*
and secure the blessings of liberty to ourselves and our posterity, do ordain and establish this Constitution for the United States of America.	*Put this passage in your own words:*

Handout B: How Much Liberty?

Directions: Think of your favorite things to do each day. Then, for items 1–3 below, fill in a favorite activity. Shade in the line below to show how much liberty you have while doing the activity. Finally, explain in 1–2 sentences why you have liberty in the activity. The first one is done for you.

Example:
Activity: **Reading a book I checked out from the library.**

| no liberty at all | a little liberty | some liberty | a lot of liberty | total liberty |

Why? I like to pick out books myself. When I have that choice, I have some liberty.

1. Activity:

| no liberty at all | a little liberty | some liberty | a lot of liberty | total liberty |

Why? _____

2. Activity:

| no liberty at all | a little liberty | some liberty | a lot of liberty | total liberty |

Why? _____

3. Activity:

| no liberty at all | a little liberty | some liberty | a lot of liberty | total liberty |

Why? _____

About the Author

After teaching for seven years, Veronica Burchard became the Director of Curriculum Development for an educational nonprofit organization near Washington, D.C. She earned her bachelor's and master's degrees in English from the University of Florida, and her interests include  American literature and civic education. Veronica lives with her husband, two sons and a very hungry guinea pig in Fairfax, Virginia.